Printed Under License ©2017 Emotional Rescue
www.emotional-rescue.com

Published by Studio Press
An imprint of Kings Road Publishing. Part of Bonnier Publishing
The Plaza, 535 King's Road, London, SW10 0SZ

www.bonnierpublishing.co.uk

Printed in Italy   10 9 8 7 6 5 4 3 2 1

The Wit & Wisdom of

DAD

Dad read the deodorant stick instructions 'Remove top and slowly push up bottom'. It was painful, but his farts smelt lovely!

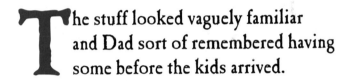

The stuff looked vaguely familiar and Dad sort of remembered having some before the kids arrived.

Dad was having a whole plethora of trouble trying to download apps!

Dad had a degree in 'Told-You-So-Ology'!

"hat would we have done without the kids?"
said Mum all gooey-eyed.
Instantly Dad's mind was filled with
images of Caribbean holidays, flash cars
and a wallet stuffed with cash.

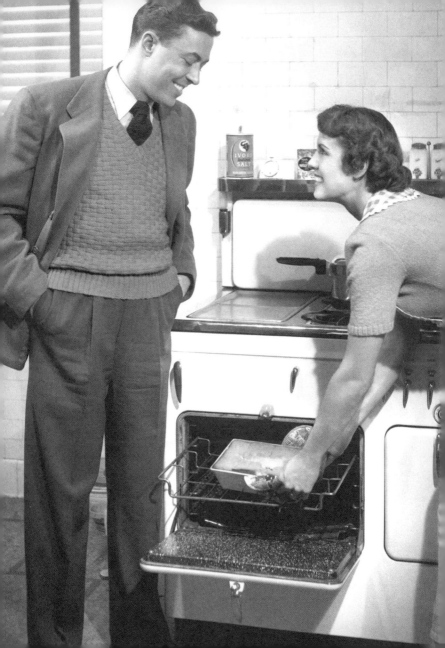

"Crikey, what on earth is that weird-looking creation called?" Dad asked.
"It's called an oven, dear!" explained Mum.

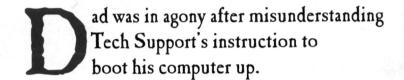

Dad was in agony after misunderstanding Tech Support's instruction to boot his computer up.

ad was really slow at DIY because he spent hours trying to remember where he'd left his pencil.

This was the type of golf course
Dad liked to play!

A Dad never stops worrying about his children's future...
what if they never leave home?!

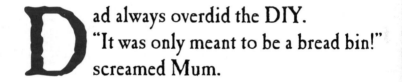

Dad always overdid the DIY.
"It was only meant to be a bread bin!"
screamed Mum.

ad was Master of the Marriage, Commander of the Family and Ruler of the Household.

So long as Mum said it was okay first.

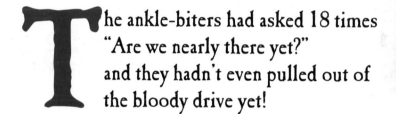

The ankle-biters had asked 18 times
"Are we nearly there yet?"
and they hadn't even pulled out of
the bloody drive yet!

The kids were just asking Dad what he'd like to do over the weekend, when his beer order turned up.

Eventually, Dad decided
to clear out
his garage.

Dad proudly holds up his child's cheque for £1.20 – the first instalment on the three billion they'd borrowed so far.

**D**ad's love of hot curries forced him to construct a fallout shelter for his family, protecting them from his regular 10 megaton nuclear fission farts.

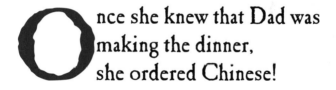Once she knew that Dad was making the dinner, she ordered Chinese!

The cheesy smile was wearing thin. When would Dad admit he'd superglued his hands to the table?

Like many teenagers, she made regular use of an automatic cash dispenser... her DAD!

Dad had got himself one of those devices that tells you when you've drank too much – commonly known as 'A Wife'.

Johnny's crying was really disrupting Dad's sleep, he had to tell Mum to get up 3 times through the night.

he main elements of Dad's diet were the four main food-groups:

1. Barley
2. Hops
3. Malt
4. Yeast

Dad was running around like a blue-arsed fly helping the family prepare for Christmas.